Contents

Introduction

Looking Inward

Looking Outward

Introduction

Do you believe that time has passed you by, your best days are behind you, or you'll never have another great opportunity? That somehow you've failed too many times to have another chance? Nothing could be further from the truth.

In this book you will find thirty-six ideas…or nuggets as I call them that will help you move decisively toward your purpose. So, don't look back, a new fulfilling journey is about to start.

Today is the best day to begin. Today is the best opportunity you have. You can still break out of your box, your comfort zone and into your new destiny.

Victor Hugo said, "Forty is the old age of youth, fifty is the youth of old age."

History is full of amazing stories of people who, no matter their circumstances, age or status in life, accomplished world-changing results. They expected to win because it's never too late to achieve your goals.

Looking Inward

#1

The most important person to talk to all day is you, so be careful what you say to you

At the age of 21, French acting legend Jeanne Moreau was told by a casting director that her head was too crooked, she wasn't beautiful enough, and she wasn't photogenic enough to make it in films. She took a deep breath and said to herself, "Alright, then, I guess I will have to make it my own way." After making nearly 100 films her own way, in 1997 she received the European Film Academy Lifetime Achievement Award.

Stop looking only at where you are and start looking at what you can be. "Our best friends and our worst enemies are our thoughts," said Dr. Frank Crane. Wrong thinking almost always leads to misery. Be careful of your thoughts. They may become words at any moment and actions very soon.

If you would like to know who is responsible for most of your troubles, take a look in the mirror. Most of the stumbling blocks people complain about are under their own hats. "Your future depends on many things, but mostly on you," said Frank Tyger.

You may succeed if nobody else believes in you, but you will never succeed if you don't believe in yourself. Zig Ziglar observes, "What you picture in your mind, your mind will go to work to accomplish. When you change your pictures you automatically change your performance." Whatever you attach consistently to the words "I am," you will become.

Gain control of your mind or it will gain control of you. Your imagination dictates your openness to positive direction. Don't build up obstacles in your imagination. Self-image sets the boundaries and limits of each of our individual accomplishments. As Charles Colton said, "We are sure to be losers when we quarrel with ourselves; it is a civil war…"

Your world first exists within you. Remember you are your own doctor when it comes to curing cold feet, a hot head and a stuffy attitude.

"Every man carries with him the world in which he must live."

-F. Marion Crawford

#2

If you can find an excuse, don't use it

No matter where you are in life, there are excuses available to stop you. The most common one that presents itself when you've reached mid-life is that every great opportunity has already passed you by. We've all heard the great story of Colonel Sanders who started Kentucky Fried Chicken when he was sixty-five. But, one of my favorites is the story about Peter Roget.

It's not that Peter Roget went through life broke. By age 61, he was an accomplished doctor, lecturer and inventor. He was a respected man of science. He was also, however, pretty insane and most definitely miserable. One thing those that knew him could agree upon—he was a tough guy to be around.

The only thing that seemed to calm him was making lists, a somewhat creepy hobby he'd had since childhood. When he retired from medicine at age 61, he realized he might as well spend all day making one huge, all-encompassing list of all the things ever—so that's exactly what he did.

Twelve years later, at age 73, Peter Roget published his giant list of words as a book, *Roget's Thesaurus of English Words and Phrases* ... otherwise known as "the thesaurus."

Roget didn't let the idea that his best opportunities were behind him stop him. His book, *Roget's Thesaurus*, has sold over 32 million copies and is still selling today…more than 150 years later.

The most unprofitable item ever manufactured is an excuse. Most failures are experts at making excuses. The world simply does not have enough crutches for all the lame excuses. It's always easier to find excuses instead of time for the things we don't want to do.

Time wasted thinking up excuses and alibis would always be better spent planning, preparing and working towards your goals in life.

"*Never* mind whom you praise, but be very careful whom you blame."

-Edmund Gosse

#3

Do not fear change, for it is an unalterable law of progress

As I write this book, I find myself at middle age. In other words, I'm in my fifties. I realize that what I've done has taken me to where I'm at, but it won't take me to where I want to be. I have to change. It's going to happen whether I want it or not. You and I can embrace it and turn it to our advantage.

What people want is progress…if they can have it without change. Impossible! You must change and recognize that change is your greatest ally. As Tryon Edwards said, "He who never changes his opinion never corrects his mistakes. …"

Change. I hope this word inspires you, rather than scares you. Herbert Spencer said, "A living thing is distinguished from a dead thing by the multiplicity of the changes at any moment taking place in it." Change is evidence of life. The truth is, life is always at some turning point.

Yesterday's formula for success is often tomorrow's recipe for failure. Consider what Thomas Watson, the founder of the IBM Corporation, said, "There is a world market for maybe five computers." Where would IBM be today if Mr. Watson had not been willing to change?

You cannot become what you are destined to be by remaining what you are. John H. Patterson said, "Only fools and dead men don't change their minds. Fools won't. Dead men can't." If you don't respect the need for change, consider this: How many things have you seen that have changed just in the past year?

When you change yourself, opportunities will change. The same kind of thinking that has brought you to where you are will not necessarily get you to where you want to go. Helen Rowland discovered this truth: "There are people whose watch stops at a certain hour and who remain permanently at that age."

I've heard it said that status quo is Latin for "the mess we're in." The man who uses yesterday's methods in today's world won't be in business tomorrow. A traditionalist is simply a person whose mind is always open to new ideas, provided they are the same old ones.

When patterns and tradition are broken, new opportunities come together. Defending your faults and errors only proves that you have no intention of quitting them. All progress is due to those who were not satisfied to let well enough alone. They weren't afraid to change. Change is not your enemy—it is your friend.

#4

You can't score a goal sitting on the sidelines

After his first audition, a casting director told actor Sidney Poitier, "Why don't you stop wasting people's time and go out and become a dishwasher or something?" It was at that moment, recalls Poitier, that he decided to devote his life to acting. He wasn't going to let someone else decide his life path.

"There's nothing in the middle of the road, but yellow stripes and dead armadillo," says Jim Hightower. Decide to do something now to make your life better. The choice is yours.

"My decision is maybe—and that's final." Is this you? Being decisive is essential for a successful life. If you deny yourself commitment, what will you do with your life? Every accomplishment, great or small, starts with a decision.

David Ambrose remarked, "If you have the will to win, you have achieved half your success; if you don't, you have achieved half your failure."

The moment you definitely commit yourself, change begins. All sorts of things happen to help you that never would have otherwise occurred. Kenneth Blanchard observed, "There is a difference between interests and commitment. When you are interested in doing something, you only do it when it is convenient. When you are committed to something, you accept no excuses, only results." Lack of decisiveness has caused more failures than lack of intelligence or ability.

Indecision often gives an advantage to others because they did their thinking beforehand. Helen Keller said, "Science may have found a cure for most evil; but it has found no remedy for the worst of them all—the apathy of human beings." Don't leave a decision for tomorrow that needs to be made today.

Remember, don't be a "middle-of-the-roader" because the middle of the road is the worst place to try to go forward. You can do everything you ought to do once you make a decision. Today, decide on your dream.

> "*Nothing* is so exhausting as indecision, and nothing is so futile."
>
> -Bertrand Russell

#5

Failure is not falling down, but staying down

The first time Jerry Seinfeld walked on-stage at a comedy club as a professional comic, he looked out at the audience, froze, and forgot the English language. He stumbled through a minute-and-a-half of material and was jeered offstage. He returned the following night and closed his set to wild applause.

The biggest mistake you can make in life is not to be true to the best you know. Follow Ralph Sockman's advice, "Give the best that you have to the highest you know—and do it now."

Mistakes are often the best teachers. The man who invented the eraser had the human race pretty well sized up. You will find that people who never make mistakes, never make anything else. Oswald Avery advises, "Whenever you fall, pick something up."

Take Paul Galvin for example. At the age of thirty-three, he had failed twice in business. He attended an auction of his own storage battery business. With his last $750, he bought back the battery eliminator portion of it. That part became Motorola. Upon his retirement in the 1960s, he quoted Ben Franklin, "Do not fear mistakes. You will know failure. Continue to reach out."

To expect life to be perfectly tailored to our specifications is to live a life of continual frustration. When you make mistakes, just learn from them and don't respond with encores. George Bernard Shaw said, "A life spent making mistakes is not only more honorable but more useful than a life spent doing nothing."

Failure is a situation, never a person. Listen to what S. I. Hayakawa said: "Notice the difference between what happens when a man says to himself, 'I failed three times,' and what happens when he says, 'I am a failure.'"

You can't travel the road to success without a puncture or two. Be like Jonah, who proved that you couldn't keep a good man down. A stumble is not a fall. In fact, a stumble may prevent a fall. Herman Melville wrote, "He who has never failed somewhere, that man cannot be great."

Thomas Edison, who failed hundreds of times before he invented the light bulb reflected, "People are not remembered by how few times they failed, but by how often they succeed."

The saddest summary of life contains three descriptions – could have, might have, and should have. If you learn from them, mistakes are useful. Cultivate this attitude and you will never be ashamed to try. Uncover the jewels from your mistakes.

"Always look at what you have left,
never look at what you have lost."

-Robert Schuller

#6

The world looks brighter behind a smile

My wife and I love to laugh. In fact, people who have known us for years have always commented about how we are always laughing. I don't know if it's my "excellent" jokes or (more likely) her wonderful sense of humor. All I know is that when you can laugh at something, you can live with it. I think it's a pretty safe bet that we've laughed every day for the thirty-five years we've been married. Hey…maybe there's a good marriage lesson.

There is a face-lift you can perform yourself that is guaranteed to improve your appearance. It is called a smile. A smile is a curve that helps us see things straight. It's a curve that you throw at another which always results in a hit. A smile goes a long way, but you're the one who must start it on its journey. So, smile often. Give your frown a rest.

Abraham Lincoln says, "Most folks are about as happy as they make up their minds to be." So cheer up. A dentist is the only person who is supposed to look down in the mouth. The worst day that you can have is the day you have not laughed.

Laughter is like changing a baby's diaper—it doesn't permanently solve any problems, but it makes things more acceptable for awhile. The optimist laughs to forget. The pessimist forgets to laugh. You might as well laugh at yourself once in awhile—everyone else does. It is the only medicine that needs no prescription, has no unpleasant taste and costs nothing.

Take to heart the words of Moshe Waldoks, "A sense of humor can help you overlook the unattractive, tolerate the unpleasant, cope with the unexpected, and smile through the unbearable." Your day goes the way the corners of your mouth turn.

I believe that every time a man smiles, and even much more so when he laughs, he adds something to his life. Janet Lane said, "Of all the things you wear, your expression is the most important."

Cheerfulness is contagious, but it seems like some folks have been vaccinated against the infection. Every man who expects to receive happiness is obligated to give happiness. You have no right to consume it without producing it. "The world is like a mirror; frown at it, and it frowns at you. Smile and it smiles, too," said Herbert Samuels.

The trouble with being a grouch is that you have to make new friends every month. The wheels of progress are not turned by cranks. As Tom Walsh says, "Every minute your mouth is turned down you lose 60 seconds of happiness." It is almost impossible to smile on the outside without feeling better on the inside.

"It was only a sunny smile,
and little it cost in the giving
but like morning light
it scattered the night
and made the day worth living."

-F. Scott Fitzgerald

#7

Do More…

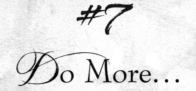

Do more than decide, discern.

Do more than consider, commit.

Do more than forgive, forget.

Do more than help, serve.

Do more than exist, live.

Do more than hear, listen.

Do more than agree, cooperate.

Do more than talk, communicate.

Do more than grow, bloom.

Do more than spend, invest.

Do more than think, create.

Do more than work, excel.

Do more than share, give.

Do more than coexist, reconcile.

Do more than think, plan.

Do more than dream, do.

Do more than see, perceive.

Do more than speak, impart.

Do more than encourage, inspire.

Do more than add, multiply.

Do more than read, apply.

Do more than receive, reciprocate.

Do more than choose, focus.

Do more than wish, believe.

Do more than advise, help.

Do more than change, improve.

Do more than reach, stretch.

#8

*A*re you a fanatic?

Let's face it. Have you ever known someone who was fabulously successful who wasn't just a little "nuts" or "crazy"? At least that's the way most less-than-successful people describe them. Your enthusiasm reflects your unexploited resources and perhaps your future.

You can succeed at almost anything for which you have limitless enthusiasm. Enthusiasm moves the world. Winston Churchill said, "Success is going from failure to failure without loss of enthusiasm." You will never rise to great truths and heights without joy and enthusiasm.

Enthusiasm must be nourished with new actions, new aspirations, new efforts and new vision. It's your own fault if your enthusiasm is gone. You have failed to feed it. "Optimism is the faith that leads to achievement," said Helen Keller. "Nothing can be done without hope or confidence."

A little girl walked to and from school daily. Though the weather that morning was questionable and clouds were forming, she made her daily trek to school. As the afternoon progressed, the winds whipped up, along with lightning. The mother of the little girl felt concerned that her daughter would be frightened as she walked home from school. She also feared the electrical storm might harm her child.

Full of concern, the mother got into her car and quickly drove along the route to her child's school. As she did, she saw her little girl walking along. At each flash of lightning, the child would stop, look up, and smile. More lightning followed quickly and with each, the little girl would stop and look at the streak of light and smile. When the mother drew up beside the child, she lowered the window and called, "What are you doing?" The child answered, "I am trying to look pretty because God keeps taking my picture." Face the storms that come your way with a smile of hope.

It isn't our position, but our disposition that makes us happy. Remember, some people freeze in the winter. Others ski. A positive attitude always creates positive results. Like Churchill says, "attitude is a little thing that makes a big difference." Depression, gloom, pessimism, despair, discouragement and fear slay more human beings than all illnesses combined.

You can't deliver the goods if your heart is heavier than the load. "We act as though comfort and luxury were the chief requirements of life, when all that we need to make us really happy is something to be enthusiastic about," said Charles Kingsley. Some people count their blessings but most think their blessings don't count.

There is a direct correlation between our passion and our potential. Being positive is essential to achievement and the foundation of true progress. If you live a life of negativity you will find yourself seasick during the entire voyage. The person who is negative is half-defeated before even beginning.

Have you ever noticed that no matter how many worries a pessimist has, he always has room for one more? Eleanor Roosevelt said, "It is better to light a candle than to curse the darkness." Das Energi reminds us to, "Vote with your life. Vote yes!"

The world belongs to the enthusiastic.

"I am an optimist.
It does not seem too much use
being anything else."

-Winston Churchill

#9

When you stretch the truth, it will snap back at you

The only way to truly be free is to be a person of truth. Truth is strong and it will prevail.

There is no limit to the height a person can attain by remaining on the level. Honesty is still the best policy. However, today there are less policyholders than there used to be. Cervantes said, "Truth will rise above falsehood as oil above water."

Though truth may not be popular, it is always right. You can't stretch the truth without making your story look pretty thin. Truth will win every argument if you stick with it long enough. The fact that nobody wants to believe something, doesn't keep it from being true.

Nothing shows dirt like a white lie. At times, a fib starts out as a little white lie, but it usually ends up as a double feature in high definition. A lie may take care of the present, but it has no future.

A Sumerian proverb says, "If you lie and then tell the truth, the truth will be considered a lie." There are no degrees of honesty. An honest man alters his ideas to fit the truth and a dishonest man alters the truth to fit his ideas.

Beware of half-truths because two half-truths do not necessarily constitute the whole truth. You may have gotten hold of the wrong half. A lie has no legs. It has to be supported by other lies. There is no acceptable substitute for honesty or a valid excuse for dishonesty. The truth is one thing for which there are no known substitutes.

"There is no power on earth more formidable than the truth."

- Margaret Lee Runbeck

#10

*P*ersistence prevails when all else fails

A father sends a small boy to bed. Five minutes later: "Da-ad ..."

"What?"

"I'm thirsty. Can you bring a drink of water?"

"No. You had your chance. Lights out."

Five minutes later: "Da-aaaad ..."

"WHAT?"

"I'm THIRSTY. Can I have a drink of water??"

"I told you NO!" If you ask again, I'll have to spank you!!"

Five minutes later: "Daaaa-aaaad ..."

"WHAT!"

"When you come in to spank me, can you bring a drink of water?"

Do you want to accomplish something in life? Be like the stonecutter. Jacob Riis says, "Look at the stone cutter hammering away at the rock, perhaps a

100 times without as much as a crack showing in it. Yet at the 101st blow it will split in two and I know it was not the last blow that did it, but all that had gone before." Whatever you want to accomplish in life will require persistence.

All things come to those who go after them. Perseverance is the result of a strong will. Stubbornness is the result of a strong "won't." Baron de Montesquieu said, "Success often depends on knowing how long it will take to succeed." This is the secret of success: never let down and never let up. Many times success consists of hanging on just one minute longer.

Persistent people always have this attitude: They never lose the game; they just run out of time. Calvin Coolidge said, "'Press on' has solved and always will solve the problems of the human race."

Determine to be something in the world and you will be something. The words "I cannot" never accomplished anything; "I will try" has wrought wonders. Keep in mind the words of Hamilton Holt: "Nothing worthwhile comes easily. Half effort does not produce half results. It produces no results. Work, continuous work and hard work, is the only way to accomplish results that last."

The truth is that persistence is a bitter plant, but it has sweet fruit. Joseph Ross said, "It takes time to succeed because success is merely the natural reward of taking time to do anything well." Victory always comes to those who persevere.

No one finds life worth living. One must make it worth living. Persistence is the quality that is most needed when it is exhausted. Often genius is just another way of spelling persistence.

"Keep on going and the chances are you will stumble on something, perhaps when you are least expecting it."

- Charles Kettering

#11

What you put off until tomorrow, you'll probably put off tomorrow, too

A mother repeatedly called upstairs for her son to get up, get dressed and get ready for school. It was a familiar routine, especially at exam time.

"I feel sick," said the voice from the bedroom.

"You are not sick. Get up and get ready," called the mother, walking up the stairs and hovering outside the bedroom door.

"I hate school and I'm not going," said the voice from the bedroom, "I'm always getting talked about behind my back, making mistakes and getting told off. Nobody likes me, and I've got no friends. And we have too many tests. It's all just pointless, and I'm not going to school ever again."

"I'm sorry, but you are going to school," said the mother through the door, continuing encouragingly, "Really, mistakes are how we learn and develop. And please try not to take criticism so personally. And I can't believe that nobody likes you—you have lots of friends at school. And yes, all those tests can be daunting, but we are all tested in many ways throughout our lives, so all of this experience at school is useful for life in general. Besides, you have to go, you are the principal."

Success comes to the man who does today what others were thinking of doing tomorrow. The lazier a man is, the more he is going to do tomorrow. "All problems become smaller if you don't dodge them, but confront them. Touch a thistle timidly, and it pricks you; grasp it boldly, and its spines crumble," said Admiral William Halsey.

Ask yourself: "If I don't take action now, what will this ultimately cost me?" When a procrastinator has finally made up his mind, the opportunity has always passed by. Here's how Edwin Markum explained it:

"When duty comes a knocking at your gate,

Welcome him in for if you bid him wait,

He will depart only to come once more

And bring seven other duties to your door."

Procrastination is the fertilizer that makes difficulties grow. When you won't start, your difficulties won't stop. Tackle any difficulty now—the longer you wait the bigger it grows. Procrastinators never have small problems because they always wait until their problems grow up.

In the game of life nothing is less important than the score at half time. The race is not always to the swift, but to those who keep on running. Robert Louis Stevenson commented, "Saints are sinners who kept on going." Some people wait so long the future is gone before they get there. Don't leave before the miracle happens!

The hardest work in the world is that which should have been done yesterday. It is usually an accumulation of easy things that should have been done last week.

Most people who sit around waiting for their ship to come in often find hardship. The things that come to a man who waits, seldom turn out to be the things he's waited for. Here's what Sir Josiah Stamp had to say, "It is easy to dodge our responsibilities, but we cannot dodge the consequences of dodging our responsibilities." People who delay action until all factors are perfect, do nothing.

A lazy person doesn't go through life—he's pushed through it. "Some day" is not a day of the week. Carve out a future; don't just whittle away the time. Wasting time wastes your life. Doing nothing is the most tiresome job in the world.

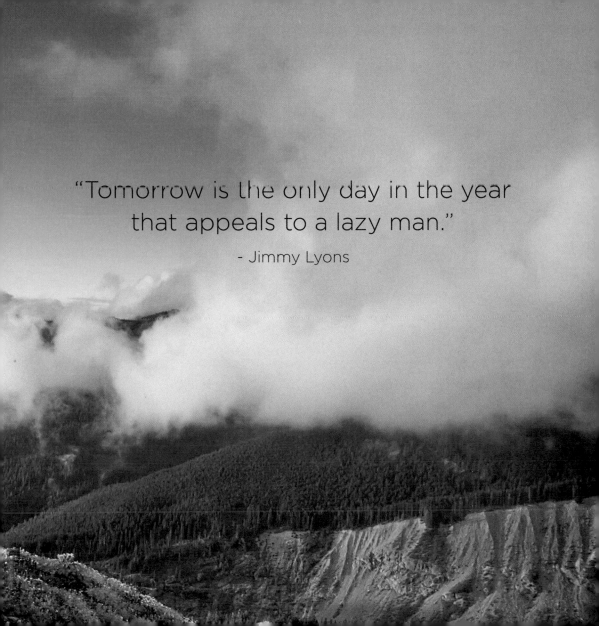

"Tomorrow is the only day in the year
that appeals to a lazy man."

- Jimmy Lyons

Questions

You can grow from asking yourself good questions. The best answers are found in asking the best questions. Here are some productive and powerful questions:

Do you believe your doubts and doubt your beliefs?

What would happen if you changed the words you spoke about your biggest problem? Your biggest opportunity?

Are you becoming ordinary?

Will people say this about your life?—"He did nothing in particular and he did it very well."

Do you tackle problems bigger than you?

Do you leave others better than you found them?

Is your favorite letter "I"?

Is it a long way from your words to your deeds?

If you try to be like him (or her), who will be like you?

Are you making dust or eating dust?

Do you count your blessings or think your blessings don't count?

Do you need a good swift kick in the seat of your "can'ts"?

Do you give up control of your life to something other than your dreams?

What kind of world would this be if everyone was just like you?

If you don't take action now, what will this ultimately cost you?

Are you a person who says, "My decision is maybe---and that's final!"

Are you known by the promises you don't keep?

Would the boy or girl you were be proud of the man or woman you are?

Are you already disappointed with the future?

In your prayers how often do you say, "And now, God, what can I do for you?"

#13

Never wish to be anything but what you are

"My mother said to me, 'If you become a soldier you'll become a general, if you become a monk you'll end up as the pope.' Instead, I became a painter and wound up as Picasso," said the great painter.

No one ever became great by imitation. Don't be a copy of something. Make your own impression.

"If God had wanted me otherwise, He would have created me otherwise," said Goethe. Dare to be what you are. Resolve to be yourself. A Congolese proverb asserts, "Wood may remain ten years in the water, but it will never become a crocodile."

Imitation is limitation. Nobody is so disappointed and so unhappy as the person who longs to be somebody other than who he or she really is. Friedrich Klopstock remarked, "He who has no opinion of his own, but depends on the opinions of others is a slave. To only dream of the person you are supposed to be is to waste the person you are."

The person who trims himself to suit everybody will soon whittle himself away. If you don't have a plan for your own life, you'll only become a part of someone else's. You can't carry two faces under one hat. "It is better to be hated for what you are, than loved for what you are not," said Andre Gide.

When you will not dare to be yourself, you will lack confidence and will crave admiration continually. You will live on the reflection of yourself in the eyes of others. "All the discontented people I know are trying to be something they are not, to do something they cannot do," said David Grayson.

There is only one life for each of us—our own. The person who walks in another's tracks never leaves his own footprints. As Doris Mortman observed, "Until you make peace with who you are, you will never be content with what you have." Most of our challenges in life come from not knowing ourselves and ignoring our best, real virtues.

Most people live their entire lives as complete strangers to themselves. Don't let that happen to you. Leo Buscaglia counseled, "The easiest thing to be in the world is you. The most difficult thing to be is what other people want you to be. Don't let them put you in that position."

The opposite of courage is not fear. It is conformity. The most exhausting and frustrating thing in life is to live it trying to be someone else.

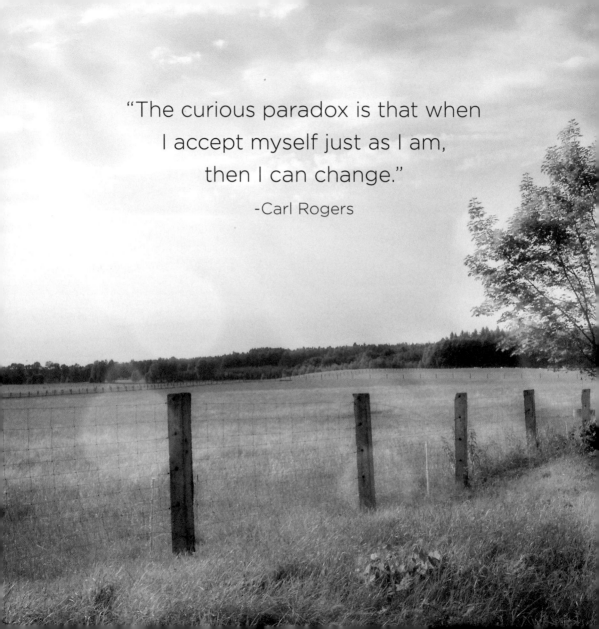

"The curious paradox is that when
I accept myself just as I am,
then I can change."

-Carl Rogers

#14

*L*aziness travels so slowly, poverty soon overtakes it

I've always admired the career of George Burns and how hard and long he worked at his craft. When he died at the age of 100 in 1996, he had spent 90 years as a comic entertainer, making numerous television and film appearances and earning an enduring popularity with his obligatory-cigar-in-hand comedy routines. His career spanned almost the entire 20th century. He did one-man shows to packed houses, getting better as he got older. He won an Academy Award for "Best Supporting Actor" in Neil Simon's The Sunshine Boys at the age of 79, the oldest recipient for the award in that category.

Approaching his eighties, he decided to start putting his wit and wisdom down on the printed page. The man who barely finished the fourth-grade ended up writing eight books—all of them best sellers. His last stage appearance was at age 97.

Here's some of his best advice:

"Don't stay in bed, unless you can make money in bed."

"Retirement at sixty-five is ridiculous. When I was sixty-five I still had pimples."

"You can't help getting older, but you don't have to get old."

"How can I die? I'm booked."

You can't reach your dream on a theory…it takes WORK. Robert Half nails it, "Laziness is the secret ingredient that goes into failure, but it's only kept a secret from the person who fails." You are made for action. It's much more natural for you to be doing than sitting.

Successful people simply take good ideas and put them into action. What free enterprise really means is the more enterprising you are the freer you become. What we need is less emphasis on free and more on enterprise.

"Nothing can come of nothing," said Shakespeare. A belief is worthless unless converted into action. The Bible is a book of faith, yet the word "work" appears in it 564 times. It's not an obscure spiritual concept. Most of the time, the answer to your prayer is: Go to work. What is it you've been dreaming about, thinking about, praying about? Is the answer staring you straight in the face? Just do something…now.

You cannot just dream yourself into what you can be. A person who wastes enormous amounts of time talking about success will win the "prize" of failure. When you're lazy, it's like working twice as hard for no results. The only time a lazy person ever succeeds is when he tries to do nothing.

Some say nothing is impossible, yet there are thousands of people doing nothing every day. The world is divided into people who do things and people who talk about doing things. Belong to the first group, there is far less competition.

Tell yourself what Brendan Francis said, "Inspirations never go on for long engagements; they demand immediate marriage to action." If the truth were known, most of our troubles arise from loafing when we should be working, and talking when we should be listening.

"There is a man in the world who is never turned down, wherever he chances to stray;

He gets the glad hand in the populous town, or out where the farmers make hay;

He is greeted with pleasure on deserts of sand, and deep in the isles of the woods;

Wherever he goes there is a welcoming hand— he's the man who delivers the goods."

-Walt Whitman

None of the secrets of success will work, unless you do.

"Striving for success without hard work
is like trying to harvest
where you haven't planted."

-David Bly

Looking Outward

#15

Hold a true friend with both of your hands

An elderly man lay dying in his bed. In death's agony, he suddenly smelled the aroma of his favorite chocolate chip cookies wafting up the stairs. He gathered his remaining strength, and lifted himself from his bed. Leaning against the wall, he slowly made his way out of his bedroom, and with even greater effort forced himself down the stairs, gripping the railing with both hands. With labored breath, he leaned against the doorframe, gazing into the kitchen.

Were it not for death's agony, he would have thought himself already in Heaven. There, spread out on newspapers on the kitchen table were literally hundreds of his favorite chocolate chip cookies. Was it Heaven? Or, was it one final act of heroic love from his devoted wife, seeing to it that he left this world a happy man?

Mustering one great final effort, he threw himself toward the table, landing on his knees in a rumpled posture. His parched lips parted. The wondrous taste of the cookie was already in his mouth, seemingly bringing him back to life. The aged, withered and shaking hand made its way to a cookie at the edge of the table, when his wife suddenly smacked it with a spatula. "Stay out of those," she said, "they're for the funeral."

The fact is not everyone will want you to succeed, no matter how hard you try. An important attribute in successful people is their impatience with negative thinking and negative-acting people.

Tell me who your friends are, and I will tell you who you are. If you run with wolves you will learn how to howl. But, if you associate with eagles, you will learn how to soar to great heights. The simple but true fact of life is that you become like those with whom you closely associate—for the good and the bad. Almost all of our sorrows spring out of relationships with the wrong people.

It's been said a good friend is like one mind in two bodies. A true friend is one who is there to care. Robert Louis Stevenson said, "A friend is a present which you give yourself." You'll find a real true friend remains a friend even when you don't deserve to have one. This friend will see you through when others think that you're through. Choose your associates carefully. What Ben Franklin said is true: "He that lies down with dogs, shall rise up with fleas." If you associate with those who are lame, you will learn how to limp.

Any time you tolerate mediocrity in others, it increases your mediocrity. We should pray, "Oh Lord, deliver me from people who talk of nothing but sickness and failure. Rather Lord, grant me the companionship of those who think success and will work for it." Anthony Robbins said, "If you ever find yourself taking two steps forward and one step backwards, invariably it's because you have mixed associations in your life." If a loafer isn't a nuisance to you, it's a sign that you are somewhat of a loafer yourself.

Never become friends with someone because you both agree on negatives. Rather, find friends who agree with you on positives. Thomas Carlyle observed, "Show me the man you honor, and I will know what kind of man you are, for it shows me what your ideal of manhood is, what kind of man you long to be."

If you were to list your greatest benefits, resources or strengths, you would find that money is one of the least important ones, while some of your greatest resources are the people you know. My friend, Mike Murdock said, "Someone is always observing you who is capable of greatly blessing you."

The way to make a true friend is to be one. Your wealth is where your friends are. A real friend is your best possession.

"Since there is nothing so well
worth having as friends,
never lose a chance to make them."

-Francesco Guicciardini

#16

When you allow other people's words to stop you, they will

Robert Sternberg received a "C" in his first college introductory psychology class. His teacher commented that "there was a famous Sternberg in psychology and it was obvious there would not be another." Three years later Sternberg graduated with honors from Stanford University with exceptional distinction in psychology, summa cum laude, and Phi Beta Kappa. In 2002, he became President of the American Psychological Association.

To succeed in life you must overcome the many efforts of others to pull you down. How you choose to respond to criticism is one of the most important decisions that you make.

The first and greatest commandment about critics is: Don't let them scare you. Lewis Carroll said, "If you limit your actions in life to things that nobody could possibly find fault with, you will not do much." Nothing significant has ever been accomplished without controversy, without criticism. When you make your mark in life, you'll always attract erasers.

Many great ideas have been lost because people who had them couldn't stand the criticism and gave up. Christopher Morley said, "The truth is, a critic is like a gong at a railroad crossing, clanging loudly and vainly as the train goes by."

A critic is simply someone who finds fault without a search warrant. It's one of the easiest things to find. William Hazlitt said, "The most insignificant people are those most apt to sneer at others. They are safe from reprisals, and have no hope of rising in their own esteem, but by lowering their neighbors." Critics not only expect the worst, but also make the worst of what happens.

Great minds discuss ideas, good minds discuss events, and small minds discuss other people. Remember this about a critic: A man who is always kicking, seldom has a leg to stand on. Dennis Wholey warned, "Expecting the world to treat you fairly because you are a good person is a little like expecting a bull not to attack you because you are a vegetarian."

Don't allow yourself to become a critic. You always make a mountain out of a molehill when you throw dirt at other people. The mud thrower never has clean hands.

You can't carve your way to success with cutting remarks. You will never move up if you are continually running someone down. I agree with John Tillotson who said, "There is no readier way for a man to bring his own worth into question than by endeavoring to detract from the worth of other men."

There's a time to respond to criticism, a time to dismiss invalid criticism and always a time to overcome our own critical nature.

Remember this, if you are afraid of criticism, you will die doing nothing. If you want a place in the sun, you have to expect some blisters and some sand kicked in your face. Criticism is a compliment when you know what you're doing is right.

"*M*en and automobiles are much alike.
Some are right at home on an uphill pull;
others run smoothly only going downgrade.
When you hear one knocking all the time,
it's a sure sign there is something wrong
under the hood."

-Henry Ford

#17

If envy were a disease, everyone would be sick

A heart surgeon took his car to his local garage for a regular service, where he usually exchanged a little friendly banter with the owner, a skilled but not especially wealthy mechanic.

"So tell me," says the mechanic, "I've been wondering about what we both do for a living, and how much more you get paid than me."

"Yes?" says the surgeon.

"Well, look at this," says the mechanic, as he worked on a big complicated engine, "I check how it's running, open it up, fix the valves, and put it all back together so it works good as new. We basically do the same job don't we? And yet you are paid ten times what I am—how do you explain that?"

The surgeon thought for a moment, and smiling gently, replied, "Try it with the engine running."

Envy is the most ridiculous of ideas, there's no single advantage to be gained from it. There is a famous old saying, "When you compare what you want with what you have, you will be unhappy. Instead, compare what you deserve with what you have and you'll discover happiness." It's not trying to keep up with the "Joneses" that causes so much trouble. It's trying to pass them. George Washington Allston reflected, "The only competition worthy of a wise man is within himself." Nothing gets you behind faster than trying to keep up with people who are already there.

If envy had a shape it would be a boomerang. Francis Bacon said, "Envy has no holidays. It has no rest." The envy that compares us to others is foolishness.

Peace comes when you stop being jealous of others. It's followed quickly with a renewed sense of purpose. Understand there will always be others prettier than you and uglier than you, richer than you and poorer than you. And so on, and so on…

What makes us discontented with our personal condition is the absurd belief that others are so much happier than we are. Helen Keller said, "Instead of comparing our lot with those who are more fortunate than we are, we should compare it with the lot of the great majority of our fellow men. It then appears that we are among the privileged." Envy consumes nothing but its own heart. It is a kind of admiration for those whom you least want to praise.

You'll find it's hard to be happier than others if you believe others to be happier than they are. Worry about what other people think of you, and you'll have more confidence in their opinion than you have in your own. Poor is the one whose pleasures depend on the permission and opinion of others.

St. Chrysostom reflected, "As a moth gnaws a garment, so doth envy consume a man." Envy provides the mud that failure throws at success. There are many roads to an unsuccessful life, but envy is the shortest of them all.

"May we never let the things we can't
have or don't have, spoil our
enjoyment of the things we
do have and can have."

-Richard L. Evans

#18

$\mathcal{M}$ake your own definition of success

Upon completing a highly dangerous tightrope walk over Niagara Falls in appalling wind and rain, The Great Zumbrati was met by an enthusiastic supporter, who urged him to make a return trip, this time pushing a wheelbarrow, which the spectator had thoughtfully brought along.

The Great Zumbrati was reluctant, given the terrible conditions, but the supporter pressed him, "You can do it. I know you can," he urged.

"You really believe I can do it?" asked Zumbrati.

"Yes, definitely, you can do it." the supporter gushed.

"Okay," said Zumbrati, "Get in the wheelbarrow..."

What you think you see in another person's life is not reality. I have a favorite saying, "Nothing is as it appears." We can't reach our destiny taking another man's road.

Judging others is a major waste of time. Judgment halts progress.

Several years ago I met with a friend whom I have known for over ten years. He looked at me and said, "John, I see all the great things that happened in your life. But, as I began to look at your life, I became full of doubt as to what was going on in my life, because I have not had the same success that you have."

I turned, looked at him and said, "Well, if it's true that you feel bad because I've done well, then would it be true that you would feel better if I had had terrible failures and had been doing much worse over the past several years?" He gave me a quizzical look and responded saying, "No, that would not be true."

I said, "Well, if it is true for one, it is true for the other. Really, it shows how inaccurate your thinking is. What happens in my life has nothing to do with what is happening in your life."

Never measure your success by what others have or haven't done. You are either a thermometer or a thermostat, registering either someone else's temperature or your own. No one can build a personal destiny upon the faith or experience of another person. As Pat Riley said, "Don't let other people tell you what you want."

Your faults will never vanish by calling attention to the faults of others. Many people have the mistaken idea that they can make themselves great by showing how small someone else is. Instead of letting their own light shine, some people spend their time trying to put out the lights of others. What a waste!

If you think you are doing better than the average person, you're an average person. Why would you want to compare yourself with someone average? Too many people seem to know how to live everybody's life but their own. We need to stop comparing ourselves to others.

"Don't take anybody else's definition
of success as your own."

- Jacqueline Briskin

#19

Forgive your enemies—
nothing will annoy them more

I've found successful people have a way of not letting things stick to them. Nothing blocks progress and innovation like a big fat grudge.

One Sunday morning before the service began, people were sitting in their pews and talking about their lives, their families, etc.... Suddenly the Devil appeared at the front of the church. Everyone started screaming and running for the front entrance, trampling each other in a frantic effort to get away from him.

Soon everyone was evacuated from the church, except for one elderly gentleman who sat calmly in his pew, not moving...seemingly oblivious to the fact that God's ultimate enemy was in his presence.

This confused Satan a bit, so he walked up to the man and said,

"Don't you know who I am?"

The man replied, "Yep, sure do."

Satan asked, "Aren't you afraid of me?"

"Nope, sure ain't," said the man.

Satan was a little perturbed at this and queried, "Why aren't you afraid of me?"

The man calmly replied, "Been married to your sister for over 48 years."

Like this elderly man, don't let stuff stick to you.

It is far better to forgive and forget than to hate and remember. Josh Billings says, "There is no revenge so complete as forgiveness."

Forgiveness is the key to personal peace. Forgiveness releases action and creates freedom. We all need to say the right thing after doing the wrong thing. Laurence Sterne said, "Only the brave know how to forgive…a coward never forgave; it is not in his nature." Josiah Bailey adds, "They who forgive most shall be most forgiven."

One of the secrets of a long and fruitful life is to forgive everybody everything every night before you go to bed. Peter von Winter said, "It is manlike to punish, but God-like to forgive." When you have a huge chip on your shoulder, it causes you to lose your balance. The heaviest thing a person can carry is a grudge.

You don't need a doctor to tell you it's better to remove a grudge than to nurse it. Forgiveness is a funny thing. It warms the heart and cools the sting.

Do you want to release the past and claim the future? Even if you're 100 percent right in a particular situation, you can be wrong when you don't forgive someone. A Yiddish proverb says, "Protest long enough that you are right and you will be wrong."

"Forgiveness does not change the past,
but it does enlarge the future."

-Paul Boese

#20

Everybody needs help from somebody

"By blood, I am Albanian. By citizenship, an Indian. By faith, I am a Catholic nun. As to my calling, I belong to the world," said Mother Teresa. She founded The Missionaries of Charity, a Roman Catholic religious congregation that in 2012 consisted of more than 4,500 sisters active in 133 countries.

For over 45 years, Mother Teresa ministered to the poor, sick, orphaned and dying. She was the recipient of numerous honors including the 1979 Nobel Peace Prize. She refused the conventional ceremonial banquet given to laureates, and asked that the $192,000 in funds be given to the poor in India. During her lifetime, Mother Teresa was named one of the top ten admired women, 18 times in a yearly Gallup poll. In 1999, a poll of Americans ranked her first in Gallup's List of "Most Widely Admired People of the 20th Century." All of this because she loved and served others.

Serving others is one of life's most awesome privileges. Albert Schweitzer said, "The only ones among you who will really be happy are those who have sought and found how to serve." Pierre Teilhard de Chardin commented,

"The most satisfying thing in life is to have been able to give a large part of one's self to others."

Hunt for the good points in people. Remember they have to do the same in your case. Then do something to help them. If you want to get ahead, be a bridge not a wall. Love others more than they deserve. Each human being presents us with an opportunity to serve. Follow the counsel of Karl Reiland who said, "In about the same degree as you are helpful you will be happy."

Too often we expect everyone else to practice the golden rule. The golden rule may be old, but it hasn't been used enough to show any signs of wear. We make a first-class mistake if we treat others as second-class people. John Andrew Holmes Jr. said, "It is well to remember that the entire population of the universe, with one trifling exception, is composed of others."

The person who sows seeds of kindness enjoys a perpetual harvest. You can't help others without helping yourself. Kindness is one of the most difficult things to give away since it usually comes back to you. Theodore C. Speers said, "You can never expect too much of yourself in the matter of giving yourself to others."

Do you want to get along better with others? Be a little kinder than necessary. A good way to forget your own troubles is to help others out of theirs.

Harry Fosdick said, "One of the most amazing things ever said on earth is Jesus' statement, 'He that is greatest among you shall be your servant.' None have one chance in a billion of being thought of as really great a century after they're gone except those who have been servants of all."

"Have you had a kindness shown?
Pass it on!
'Twas not given for thee alone,
Pass it on!

Let it travel down the years,
Let it wipe another's tears,
'Till in heaven the deed appears
Pass it on!"

-Henry Burton

#21

Opportunity is where you are, never where you were

Tom Landry, Chuck Noll, Bill Walsh, and Jimmy Johnson accounted for 11 of the 19 Super Bowl victories from 1974 to 1993. They also share the distinction of having the worst records of first-season head coaches in NFL history—they didn't win a single game. If any of these men focused on where they had been instead of where they were going, none of them would have made it to the Hall of Fame.

Most people tend to overrate that which they don't possess and underrate what they have. Edgar Watson Howe said, "People are always neglecting something they can do in trying to do something they can't do." I agree with Teddy Roosevelt when he said, "Do what you can, with what you have, where you are." The only way to learn anything thoroughly is by starting at the bottom (except when learning how to swim). To be successful, do what you can.

To get anywhere you must launch out for somewhere or you will get nowhere. Hamilton Wright Mabie said, "The question for each man to settle is not what he would do if he had the means, time, influence and educational advantages, but what he will do with the things he has."

The truth is that many are successful because they didn't have the advantages others had. People with enterprise accomplish more than others because they go ahead and do it before they are ready. The best place to start is where you are. Ken S. Keyes, Jr. said, "To be upset over what you don't have is to waste what you do have."

No improvement is as certain as that which proceeds from the right and timely use of what you already have.

The truth is, you can't know what you can do until you try. The most important thing about reaching your dream is starting right where you are. Edward Everett Hale said, "…I cannot do everything, but I still can do something; and because I cannot do everything, I will not refuse to do something I can do."

Everyone who has arrived had to begin where they were.

"No longer forward nor behind I look in hope or fear; But, grateful, take the good I find, The best of now and here."

-John Greenleaf Whittier

#22

The past is always going to be the way it was

After Carl Lewis won the gold medal for the long jump in the 1996 Olympic Games, he was asked to what he attributed his longevity, having competed for almost 20 years. He said, "Remembering that you have both wins and losses along the way. I don't take either one too seriously."

There is no future in the past. Stop trying to change it. Your future contains more happiness than any past you can remember. Believe that the best is yet to come.

If you look back too much, you'll soon be heading that way. Your destiny is forward, never backward. Katherine Mansfield advised, "Make it a rule of life never to regret and never to look back. Regret is an appalling waste of energy. You can't build on it. It's only good for wallowing in."

You are more likely to make mistakes when you act only on past experiences. Rosy thoughts about the future can't exist when your mind is full of the blues about the past.

Are you backward about going forward? Phillip Raskin said, "The man who wastes today lamenting yesterday will waste tomorrow lamenting today." Squash the "good old days" bug.

The more you look back, the less you will get ahead. Thomas Jefferson was right when he said, "I like the dreams of the future better than the history of the past." Many a "has-been" lives on the reputation of his reputation.

When depressed, you will find that it is because you are living in the past. What's a sure sign of stagnation in your life? When you dwell on the past at the expense of the future, you stop growing and start dying. Hubert Humphrey mused, "The good old days were never that good, believe me. The good new days are today, and better days are coming tomorrow. Our greatest songs are still unsung."

Never let yesterday use up too much of today. It's true what David McNally said, "Your past cannot be changed, but you can change your tomorrow by your actions today." The first rule for happiness is: Avoid lengthy thinking about the past. Nothing is as far away as one hour ago.

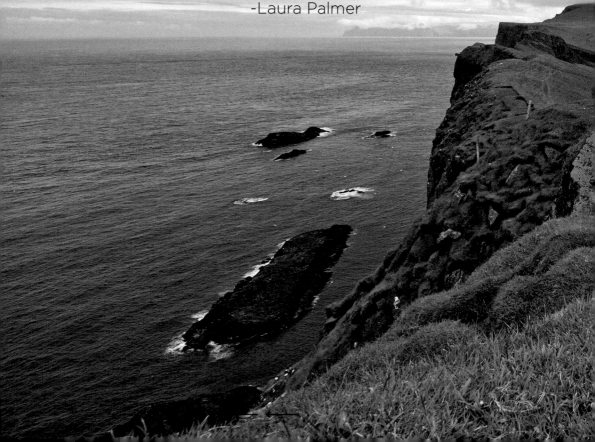

"Don't waste today regretting yesterday instead of making a memory for tomorrow."

-Laura Palmer

#23

Don't go through your life too fast

A young and successful executive was traveling down a neighborhood street, going a bit too fast in his new Jaguar. He was watching for kids darting out from between parked cars and slowed down when he thought he saw something.

As his car passed, no children appeared. Instead, a brick smashed into the Jag's side door! He slammed on the brakes and drove the Jag back to the spot where the brick had been thrown. The angry driver then jumped out of the car, grabbed the nearest kid and pushed him up against a parked car, shouting, "What was that all about and who are you? Just what the heck are you doing? That's a new car and that brick you threw is going to cost a lot of money. Why did you do it?"

The young boy was apologetic. "Please mister...please, I'm sorry...I didn't know what else to do," he pleaded. "I threw the brick because no one else would stop..."

With tears dripping down his face and off his chin, the youth pointed to a spot just around a parked car. "It's my brother," he said. "He rolled off the curb and fell out of his wheelchair and I can't lift him up."

Now sobbing, the boy asked the stunned executive, "Would you please help me get him back into his wheelchair? He's hurt and he's too heavy for me."

Moved beyond words, the driver tried to swallow the rapidly swelling lump in his throat. He hurriedly lifted the handicapped boy back into the wheelchair, then took out his fancy handkerchief and dabbed at the fresh scrapes and cuts. A quick look told him everything was going to be okay.

"Thank you and may God bless you," the grateful child told the stranger. Too shook up for words, the man simply watched the little boy push his wheelchair-bound brother down the sidewalk toward their home.

It was a long, slow walk back to the Jaguar. The damage was very noticeable, but the driver never bothered to repair the dented side door. He kept the dent there to remind him of this message: Don't go through life so fast that someone has to throw a brick at you to get your attention!

Your success has little to do with speed, but more to do with timing and direction. What benefit is running if you're on the wrong road? The key is doing the right thing at the right time. Tryon Edwards said, "Have a time and place for everything, and do everything in its time and place, and you will not only accomplish more, but have far more leisure than those who are always hurrying…" The problem is that many a go-getter never stops long enough to let opportunity catch up with him.

The way to the top is neither swift nor easy. Nothing worthwhile ever happens in a hurry—so be patient. The less patience a person has the more he loses it.

When you don't have the right timing, you will sow hurry and reap frustration. As Gandhi said, "There is more to life than simply increasing its speed." The trouble with life in the fast lane is that you get to the other end too soon.

Haste makes waste: give time time. If the time has passed, preparation does no good. Many people overestimate what they can do in a year and underestimate what they can do in a lifetime.

Many times the action that you take at the right time has no immediate relationship to the answer—it's to get you to the right place at the right time.

Jean de la Bruyere said, "There is no road too long to the man who advances deliberately and without undue haste; no honor is too distant to the man who prepares himself for them with patience."

We are happiest when we discover that what we should be doing and what we are doing are the same things. You will never be what you ought to be until you are doing what you ought to be doing. Do what's right, the right way, at the right time.

If you are facing the right direction, just keep on walking. Adopt the right pace; if you go too fast, you will catch up with misfortune. If you go too slowly; misfortune will catch up with you.

"Failure at a task may be the result of having tackled it at the wrong time."

-Brendan Francis

#24

*K*eep learning, keep growing

My friend, the late Brian Klemmer used to begin many of his seminars by holding up a $100 bill. In a room of 200, he asked, "Who would like this $100 bill?"

Hands started going up.

He said, "I am going to give this $100 to one of you but first, let me do this." He proceeded to crumple the dollar bill up.

He then asked, "Who still wants it?"

Still the hands were up in the air.

"Well," he replied, "What if I do this?" And he dropped it on the ground and started to grind it into the floor with his shoe.

He picked it up, now all crumpled and dirty. "Now who still wants it?" Still the hands went into the air.

"My friends, you have all learned a very valuable lesson. No matter what I did to the money, you still wanted it because it did not decrease in value. It was still worth $100.

Many times in our lives, we are dropped, crumpled, and ground into the dirt by the decisions we make and the circumstances that come our way. We feel as though we are worthless. But no matter what has happened or what will happen, you will never lose your value.

Have you ever noticed there are people you know who are literally at the same place today as they were five years ago? They still have the same dreams, the same problems, the same alibis, the same opportunities and the same way of thinking. They are standing still in life.

Many people literally unplug their clocks at a certain point in time and stay at that fixed moment the rest of their lives. We're designed to grow, to continue to learn and improve. The biggest room in our house is always the room for self-improvement.

John Wooden said, "It's what you learn after you know it all that counts." I must admit that I am somewhat of a fanatic about this. I hate to have idle time—time in which I am not learning anything. Those around me know that I must always have something to read or to write during any idle moment that might arise. I know what Margaret Fuller said to be true: "Today a reader, tomorrow a leader."

In fact, I try to learn from everyone. From one, I may learn what not to do, while from another, I learn what to do. Learn from the mistakes of others. You can never live long enough to make all the mistakes yourself. You can learn more from a wise man when he is wrong than a fool who is right.

Goethe said, "Everybody wants to be somebody; nobody wants to grow." An important way to keep growing is to never stop asking questions. The person who is afraid of asking is ashamed of learning. Only hungry minds can grow.

Harvey Ullman said, "Anyone who stops learning is old, whether this happens at 20 or 80. Anyone who keeps on learning not only remains young, but becomes consistently more valuable regardless of physical capacity."

Learn from others. Learn to see in the challenges of others, the ills you should avoid. Experience is a present possession that keeps us from repeating the past in the future. Life teaches us by giving us new problems before we solve the old ones. Think education is expensive or difficult? Listen to Derek Bok: "If you think education is expensive—try ignorance."

"You will never change your actions until you change your mind."

-Van Crouch

#25

$\mathscr{F}$ind a giant and slay it

My first book had just been released. I was excited and was privately hoping it would sell 10,000 copies. Since I was in the publishing business, I knew this was an adventurous goal, because most books only sell a few thousand copies. I was unknown, with no platform and the odds were even greater against me...until I talked to Pat Judd.

I vividly remember telling him privately my dream to sell 10,000 books. And his instant response, "I'll be disappointed if it doesn't sell 100,000." I literally could feel my limits come off. I would never look at my books the same way. I went beyond my limited thinking. (The rest of the story...that book sold over 600,000 copies!)

Be involved in something bigger than you. We should eagerly want to do what takes us out of our comfort zone. Be like David. Find a Goliath and slay it. Always pick an obstacle big enough to matter when you overcome it.

Until you give yourself to some great cause, you haven't really begun to fully live. Henry Miller said, "The man who looks for security, even in the mind, is like a man who would chop off his limbs in order to have artificial ones which will give him no pain or trouble." Nothing significant is ever accomplished by a realistic person.

Tradition offers no hope for the present and makes no preparation for the future. Day by day, year by year, broaden your horizons. Russell Davenport remarked, "Progress in every age results only from the fact that there are some men and women who refuse to believe that what they knew to be right cannot be done."

Know the rules and then break some. Take the lid off as Melvin Evans said: "The men who build the future are those who know that greater things are yet to come, and that they themselves will help bring them about. Their minds are illuminated by the blazing sun of hope. They never stop to doubt. They haven't time."

If you really want to defend what you believe, live it. Do a right about face that turns you from failure to success. Keep this formula in mind: Always act as if it's impossible to fail. One of the greatest pleasures you can find is doing what people say you cannot do.

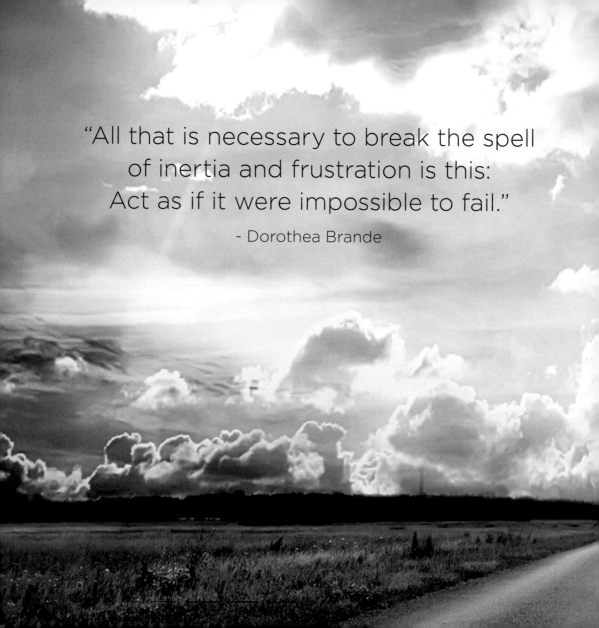

Go From...

Go from whining to winning.

Go from lukewarm to "on fire."

Go from security to opportunity.

Go from fear to faith.

Go from resisting to receiving.

Go from thinking of yourself to thinking of others.

Go from complaining to obtaining.

Go from drifting to steering.

Go from burnout to recharged.

Go from failure to learning.

Go from regrets of the past
to dreams of the future.

Go from frustrated to focused.

Go from prejudice to reconciliation.

Go from ordinary to extraordinary.

Go from defective to effective.

Go from despiteful to insightful.

Go from being a problem to being an answer.

Go from trying to committing.

Go from a copy to an original.

Go from envying others to serving others.

Go from ingratitude to thanksgiving.

Go from faultfinding to forgiveness.

Go from criticism to compliments.

Go from alibis to action.

Go from procrastination to progress.

Go from hesitation to obedience.

Go from blending in to standing out.

Go from fractured to focused.

Go from taking to giving.

Go from wishing to wisdom.

Go from quitting to starting.

Go from late to great!

#27

Are you drifting toward an uncertain future?

You can predict your future by the awareness you have of your purpose. Too many people know what they are running from, but not what they are running to. First, concentrate on finding your purpose, then concentrate on fulfilling it. Having a powerful why will provide you with the necessary how. Purpose, not money, is your real asset.

Take care of your purpose and the end will take care of itself. When you base your life on principle, 99 percent of your decisions are already made. Purpose does what it must; talent does what it can. Considering an action? Listen to Marcus Aurelius, "Without a purpose nothing should be done."

As you reach for your destiny, it will be like a magnet that pulls you, not like a brass ring that only goes around once. Destiny draws. "The height of your accomplishments will equal the depth of your convictions. Seek happiness for its own sake, and you will not find it; seek for purpose and happiness will follow as a shadow comes with the sunshine," said William Scolavino.

You're not truly free until your supreme mission in life has made you captive. As John Foster said, "It is a poor disgraceful thing not to be able to reply, with some degree of certainty, to the simple questions, 'what will you be? What will you do?'"

There is something for you to start that is destined for you to finish. As individuals go their right way, destiny accompanies them. Don't part company with your destiny. It is an anchor in the storm. A purposeless life is an early death.

What you believe is the force that determines what you accomplish or fail to accomplish in life. It's just as H. L. Mencken said, "You can't do anything about the length of your life, but you can do something about its width and depth."

The average person's life consists of 20 years of having parents ask where he or she is going, 40 years of having a spouse ask the same question and at the end, the mourners wondering the same thing. Martin Luther King Jr. said, "If a man hasn't discovered something that he will die for, he isn't fit to live." Abandon yourself to destiny.

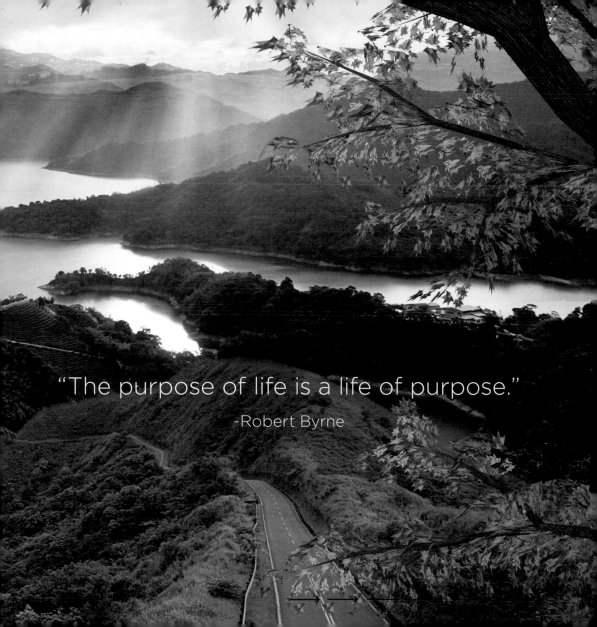

"The purpose of life is a life of purpose."

-Robert Byrne

#28

Know the real value of today

Doing your best at this moment puts you in the best place for the next moment. When can you live if not now? All the flowers of tomorrow are in the seeds of today. Ellen Metcalf remarked, "There are many people who are at the right place at the right time but don't know it." It is okay to take time to plan, but when the time of action has arrived, stop thinking and go for it! Noah didn't wait for his ship to come in—he built one!

Here's a story that brings this point home. A young man was getting ready to graduate college. For many months he had admired a beautiful sports car in a dealer's showroom, and knowing his father could well afford it, he told him that was all he wanted.

As graduation day approached, the young man awaited signs that his father had purchased the car. Finally, on the morning of his graduation his father called him into his private study. His father told him how proud he was to have such a fine son, and told him how much he loved him. He handed his son a beautifully wrapped gift box.

Curious, but somewhat disappointed the young man opened the box and found a lovely, leather-bound Bible. Angrily, he raised his voice at his father and said, "With all your money you give me a Bible?" and stormed out of the house, leaving the holy book.

Many years passed and the young man was very successful in business. He had a beautiful home and wonderful family, but realized his father was very old, and thought perhaps he should go to him. He had not seen him since that graduation day. Before he could make arrangements, he received a telegram telling him his father had passed away, and willed all of his possessions to his son. He needed to come home immediately and take care of things. When he arrived at his father's house, sudden sadness and regret filled his heart.

He began to search his father's important papers and saw the still new Bible, just as he had left it years ago. With tears, he opened the Bible and began to turn the pages. As he read those words, a car key dropped from an envelope taped behind the Bible. It had a tag with the dealer's name, the same dealer who had the sports car he had desired. On the tag was the date of his graduation, and the words...PAID IN FULL.

How many times do we miss a blessing in our life because they are not packaged as we expected?

Seize the moment! Today was once the future from which you expected so much in the past. As Horatio Dresser said, "The ideal never comes. Today is ideal for him who makes it so." Live for today. Don't let what you have within your grasp today be missed entirely because only the future intrigued you and the past disheartened you.

"Write it on your heart that every day is the best day of the year," said Ralph Waldo Emerson. The most important thing in our lives is what we are doing now. The future that you long and dream for begins today.

The regrets that most people experience in life come from failing to act when opportunity presents itself. Albert Dunning said, "Great opportunities come to all, but many do not know that they have met them. The only preparation to take advantage of them is…to watch what each day brings."

Today, well lived, will prepare you for both the opportunities and obstacles of tomorrow. I agree with Marcus Valerius Martialis when he said, "Tomorrow life is too late; live today."

Few know when to rise to the occasion. Most only know when to sit down. Many spend too much time dreaming of the future, never realizing that a little of it arrives every day.

"Every day comes bearing its own gifts.
Untie the ribbons."

- Ruth Ann Schabacker

#29

If you don't risk anything you risk even more

Babe Ruth is famous for his past home run record, but for decades he also held the record for strikeouts. He hit 714 home runs and struck out 1,330 times in his career (about which he said, "Every strike brings me closer to the next home run."). So swing for the fence!

For many years "safety first" has been the motto of the human race…but it has never been the motto of leaders. Herbert Casson said, "A leader must face danger. He must take the risk and the blame and the brunt of the storm." If you want to be successful, you must either have a chance or take one. You can't get your head above water if you never stick your neck out.

As Elizabeth Kenny reflected, "It is better to be a lion for a day than a sheep all your life." If you dare for nothing, you need hope for nothing.

Every person has a chance to improve himself, but some just don't believe in taking chances. I agree with Lois Platford when she said, "You have all eternity to be cautious in when you're dead." Being destined for greatness requires you to take risks and confront great hazards.

No one reaches the top without daring. "You'll always miss 100 percent of the shots that you don't take," said Wayne Gretsky. A dream that does not include risk is not really worthy of being called a dream. If you'll never take risks, you'll never accomplish great things. Everybody dies, but not everyone has lived. Edward F. Halifax said, "He who leaves nothing to chance will do few things poorly, but he will do few things."

If you have found yourself throughout life never scared, embarrassed, disappointed or hurt, it means you have never taken any chances.

Believe in taking chances and you will improve yourself. Robert F. Kennedy said, "Only those who dare to fail greatly can achieve greatly."

Whenever you see a successful person, I guarantee that person took risks and made courageous decisions. Success favors the bold. The world is a book where those who do not take risks read only one page. As David Mahoney said, "Refuse to join the cautious crowd that plays not to lose. Play to win."

"If your life is ever going to get better,
you'll have to take risks.
There is simply no way you can grow
without taking chances."

- David Viscott

#30

The time is always right to do the right thing

You achieve according to what you believe. Here's how Richard Huseman described it, "Be driven by excellence. To be driven by excellence that at the end of each day, each month, each year, and indeed at the end of life itself, we must ask one important question: Have we demanded enough of ourselves, and by our example, inspired those around us to put forth their best effort and achieve their greatest potential?"

More harm has been done by weak people than by wicked people. The problems of this world have been caused by the weakness of goodness rather than by the strength of evil. The true measure of a person is the height of his ideals, the breadth of his sympathy, the depth of his convictions, and the length of his patience. Eddie Rickenbacker encouraged us to: "Think positively and masterfully, with confidence and faith, and life becomes more secure, more fraught with action, richer in achievement and experience."

The right train of thought will take you to a better station in life. Stand for what's right, and then you win, even if it looks like you've lost.

One secret of success is being able to put your best foot forward without stepping on anybody's toes. "Success is peace of mind, which is a direct result of self-satisfaction in knowing you did your best to become the best that you are capable of becoming," said Coach John Wooden.

Elevate your personal standards of quality. Whatever you thought was good enough for now, add 10 percent more. Better is better.

"The roots of true achievement lie in the will to become the best that you can become."

-Harold Taylor

#31

$\mathcal{N}$o focus, no peace. Know focus, know peace

We know that Walt Disney was successful. Maybe the key to his success is found in his confession, "I love Mickey Mouse more than any woman I've ever known." Now, that's focus!

George Bernard Shaw wrote, "Give a man health and a course to steer, and he will never stop to trouble about whether he is happy or not." Ask yourself this question, "What am I really aiming at?"

Delegate, simplify or eliminate low priorities as soon as possible. Do more by doing less. As James Liter said, "One thought driven home is better than three left on base."

There are too many people in too many cars, in too much of a hurry, going too many directions, to get nowhere for nothing. "There is so little time for the discovery of all that we want to know about things that really interest us. We cannot afford to waste it on things that are only of casual concern for us, or in which we are interested only because other people have told us what we ought to be," said Alec Waugh. For the person who has no focus, there is no peace.

A famous old saying says it well, "If you chase two rabbits, both will escape." Don't be a jack-of-all-trades and a master of none. What you set your heart on will determine how you will spend your life.

How can you get what you want? William Locke answered, "I can tell how to get what you want; you just got to keep a thing in view and go for it, and never let your eyes wander to the right or left or up or down. And looking back is fatal."

I believe you will only find happiness when you are going somewhere wholeheartedly, in one direction without regret or reservation. Do what you are doing while you are doing it. The more complicated you are, the more ineffective you will become.

As tennis legend Vic Braden said, "Losers have tons of variety. Champions take pride in just learning to hit the same old boring winners." The quickest way to do many things is to do only one thing at a time. The only ones who will be remembered are those who have done one thing superbly well. Don't be like the man who said, "I'm focused, it's just on something else."

#32

Dare to go further than you can see

There's a legendary story illustrating the difference between positive thinking and negative thinking:

Many years ago a British shoe manufacturer sent two salesmen to Africa to investigate and report back on market potential. The first salesman reported back, "There is no potential here—nobody wears shoes."

The second salesman reported back, "There is massive potential here—nobody wears shoes." This simple short story provides one of the best examples of how a single situation may be viewed in two quite different ways—negatively or positively.

It could be argued that Wayne Gretsky is the greatest hockey player in history. Asked about his secret for continuing to lead the national hockey league in goals year after year, Gretsky replied, "I skate to where the puck is going to be, not where it has been."

Too many people expect little, ask little, therefore receive little and are content with little. I sincerely believe that we would accomplish many more things if we did not so automatically view them as impossible.

Don't do anything that doesn't require faith. Those who dare, do; those who dare not, do not. Isak Dinesen said, "God made the world round so that we would never be able to see too far down the road."

You have reached stagnation when all you ever exercise is caution. Sometimes you must press ahead despite the pounding fear in your head that says, "Turn back."

"Who dares nothing,
need hope for nothing."

-Friedrich Schiller

#33

The more you worry about the future, the less you'll know what to do with it

Scott Williams shares this story. Ron Wayne was one of the original co-founders of Apple—along with Steve Jobs and Steve Wozniak (Woz), the original Apple-founding trifecta. Wayne is actually responsible for designing the company's original logo. The Apple logo has evolved into what we have come to know as the forbidden fruit that looks like Adam or Eve took a bite. Wayne also wrote the original Apple manual and drew up the start-up company's partnership agreement.

Wayne set himself up for financial success and the original agreement gave him a 10 percent ownership stake in Apple, a position that would be worth $22 billion dollars today if Wayne had held onto it. Instead of holding onto it, Wayne dropped it like it was hot. Oops, bad move!

According to *Mercury News*, Wayne was afraid that Jobs' wild spending and Woz's life of bling before bling was bling would cause Apple to flop. Wayne decided to step down from his role of being the "mature one" in the bunch. Wayne took a bite out of Apple and left the company after only 11 days. He was a little more worried than Jobs or Woz because he was the only one of the three founders with assets that creditors could seize; he sold back his shares for $800. Let me repeat that last line…Wayne sold his shares for $800.

One of the best discoveries you can make is to find you can do what you were afraid you couldn't do.

Sister Mary Tricky said, "Fear is faith that it won't work out." So, never take the advice of your fears. John Adams said it best, "Never trouble trouble until trouble troubles you."

Fears, like babies, grow larger by nursing them. Fear wants to grow faster than teenagers. As Benjamin Disraeli says, "Nothing in life is more remarkable than the unnecessary anxiety which we endure, and generally create ourselves." We must act in spite of fear… not because of it.

Worry doesn't help tomorrow's troubles, but it does ruin today's happiness. As John Lubbock said, "A day of worry is more exhausting than a week of work." But, the truth is, more people worry about the future than prepare for it.

Only your mind can produce fear. We choose our joys and our fears long before we experience them. Fears lie and make us not go where we might have won. Arthur Roche described it this way, "Worry is a thin stream of fear trickling through the mind. If encouraged, it cuts a channel into which all other thoughts are drained." Instead, do what Dr. Rob Gilbert advised, "It's all right to have butterflies in your stomach. Just get them to fly in formation."

There are always two voices sounding in our ears—the voice of fear and the voice of faith. Never let your fears hold you back from pursuing your dream. If you are afraid to step up to the plate, you will never hit a home run.

Shakespeare wrote, "Our doubts are traitors, and they make us lose what we oft might win, by fearing to attempt." Worry never fixes anything.

"Don't roll up your pant legs
before you get to the stream."

-Emanuel Celler

#34

Don't give until it hurts, give until it feels good

The expression, "die empty" has been one that's inspired me, but also challenged me. You see, I'm not a natural giver. It's not that I don't believe in giving…it's just more fun (it seems) to keep as much as you can.

But by now, I have discovered that the true secret to living is giving. Charles Spurgeon said, "Feel for others—in your wallet." In fact, the best generosity is that which is quick. When you give quickly, it is like giving twice. The fact is—the good that happens in your life is not so you can keep it to yourself—it's so you can share it with others. When you give only after being asked, you have waited too long. As an Indian proverb says, "Good people, like clouds, receive only to give away."

A good way to judge a man is by what he says. A better way is by what he does. The best way is by what he gives. "Blessed are those who can give without remembering and take without forgetting," said Elizabeth Bibesco. The big problem is not the "haves" and "have-nots"—it's the "give-nots." The Lord loves a cheerful giver—and so does everyone else.

Giving is always the thermometer of our love. "When you cease to make a contribution, you begin to die," said Eleanor Roosevelt. When you live for another, it's the best way to live for yourself. John Wesley advised, "Make all you can, save all you can, give all you can." That's a good formula for a successful life.

When it comes to giving, some people stop at nothing. Greed always diminishes what has been gained. As Mike Murdock says, "Giving is proof that you have conquered greed." The trouble with too many people who give until it hurts is that they are so sensitive to pain.

If you have, give. If you lack, give. As James Allen said, "The law of the harvest is to reap more than you sow..." The test of generosity is not necessarily how much you give, but how much you have left.

Go ahead and die empty because what you give lives.

"There is no happiness in having or in getting, but only in giving."

-Henry Drummond

#35

Turn an obstacle to your advantage

Beethoven handled the violin awkwardly and preferred playing his own compositions instead of improving his technique. His teacher called him "hopeless as a composer." And, of course, you know that he wrote five of his greatest symphonies while completely deaf.

Adversity has its advantages. The door to opportunity swings on the hinges of opposition. Problems are the price of progress. The obstacles of life are intended to make us better, not bitter. Caleb Colton described it this way: "Times of general calamity and confusion have ever been productive of the greatest minds. The purest ore is produced from the hottest furnace, and the brightest thunderbolt is elicited from the darkest storm."

Obstacles are merely a call to strengthen, not quit your resolve to achieve worthwhile goals. Bob Harrison says, "Between you and anything significant will be giants in your path." The truth is, if you like things easy, you will have difficulties. If you like problems, you will succeed.

If you have a dream without aggravations, you don't really have a dream. Have the attitude of Louisa May Alcott who said, "I am not afraid of storms for I am learning how to sail my ship." It seems that great trials are the necessary preparation for greatness. The Chinese have a proverb that says, "The gem cannot be polished without friction, nor man perfected without trials."

I've discovered for every obstacle you face, there is an answer. Mike Murdock said, "If God cushioned every blow, you would never learn to grow." Instead, don't let your problems take the lead. You take the lead. The problem you face is simply an opportunity for you to do your best.

What attitude do we need to have toward difficulties? Lou Holtz advised, "Adversity is another way to measure the greatness of individuals. I never had a crisis that didn't make me stronger."

You will find that when you encounter obstacles you will discover things about yourself that you never really knew. Challenges make you stretch— they make you go beyond the norm. Turning an obstacle to your advantage is the first necessary step towards victory.

Life, I believe, promises a safe landing, but not a calm voyage. It is as uncertain as a grapefruit's squirt. Consider what Sydney Harris said, "When I hear somebody say that 'Life is hard,' I am always tempted to ask, 'Compared to what?'" We might as well face our problems. We can't run fast or far enough to get away from them all. Rather, we should have the attitude of Stan Musial, the famous Hall of Fame baseball player, who when commenting on how to handle a spitball said, "I'll just hit the dry side of the ball." The breakfast of champions is not cereal, it's obstacles.

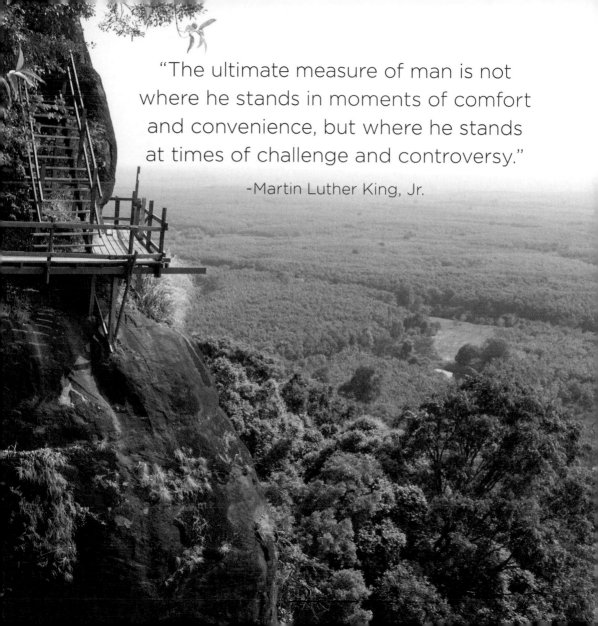

"The ultimate measure of man is not where he stands in moments of comfort and convenience, but where he stands at times of challenge and controversy."

-Martin Luther King, Jr.

#36

Go where you have never gone before

On Lake Isabella, located in the high desert, an hour east of Bakersfield, California, some folks, new to boating, were having a problem. No matter how hard they tried, they couldn't get their brand new 22-foot Bayliner to perform. It wouldn't stay level, and it was very sluggish in almost every maneuver, no matter how much power was applied.

After about an hour of trying to make it go, they putted to a nearby marina, thinking someone there could tell them what was wrong. A thorough topside check revealed everything was in perfect working condition.

The engine ran fine, the outdrive went up and down, the prop was the correct size and pitch. So, one of the marina guys jumped in the water to check underneath. He came up choking on water, he was laughing so hard.

Under the boat, still strapped securely in place, was the trailer. What unknown limits are holding you back?

Dare to think unthinkable thoughts. Pearl Buck said, "All things are possible until they are proved impossible—even the impossible may only be so as of now." Somebody is always doing what somebody else said couldn't be done.

Life is too short to think small. Rather do as Pastor Joel Budd encourages us to do, "March off the map." Most people could do more than they think they can, but they usually do less than they think they can. You never know what you cannot do until you try. Everything is possible—never use the word "never." Charles Schwab said, "When a man has put a limit on what he will do, he has put a limit on what he can do."

Never tell a young person that something cannot be done. Mankind may have been waiting for centuries for somebody ignorant enough of the impossible to do that thing. If you devalue your dreams, rest assured the world won't raise the price. You will find that great leaders are rarely "realistic" by other people's standards.

Damon Runyan says, "You only become a winner if you are willing to walk over the edge." Take the lid off. Know your limits—then ignore them!

When you climb the tallest tree, you win the right to the best fruit. Gloria Swanson said, "Never say never…Never is a long, undependable thing, and life is too full of rich possibilities to have restrictions placed upon it."

To believe an idea impossible is to make it so. Consider how many fantastic projects have miscarried because of small thinking or have been strangled in their birth by a cowardly imagination. I like what Gabriel Victor Mirabeau said. When he heard the word "impossible," he responded, "Never let me hear that foolish word again."

Develop an infinite capacity to ignore what others think can't be done. Don't just grow where you are planted. Bloom where you are planted and bear fruit.

Daniel Webster said, "There is always room at the top." No one can predict to what heights you can soar. Even you will not know until you spread your wings.

The answer to your future lies outside the confines you have right now. I like to put it this way; If you want to see if you can really swim, don't frustrate yourself with shallow water. Cavett Robert said, "Any man who selects a goal in life which can be fully achieved has already defined his own limitations." Rather be as Art Sepulveda said, "Be a history maker and a world shaker."

You've learned to expect to win
because it's never too late
to achieve your goals!!

About the Author

 John Mason is a national best-selling author, noted speaker and executive author coach. He is the founder and president of Insight International, an organization dedicated to helping people reach their dreams and fulfill their destinies.

He has authored 14 books including *An Enemy Called Average, You're Born An Original-Don't Die A Copy,* and *Know Your Limits—Then Ignore Them* which have sold over 1.4 million copies and been translated into 30 languages throughout the world. These books are widely known as a source of sound wisdom, genuine motivation and practical principles. His writings have been published in *Reader's Digest,* along with numerous other national and international publications.

Known for his quick wit, powerful thoughts and insightful ideas, he's a popular speaker across the U.S. and around the world.

John and his wife, Linda, have four children: Michelle, Greg, Michael and David. They reside in Tulsa, Oklahoma.

John Mason welcomes the opportunity to speak for your business or organization. He's a very popular communicator on a variety of topics, including leadership, motivation and success.

John Mason
www.freshword.com
contact@freshword.com
Insight International
P.O. Box 54996
Tulsa, OK 74155

If you have enjoyed this book, we invite you to check out our entire collection of gift books with free inspirational movies, at www.simpletruths.com. You'll discover it's a great way to inspire friends and family, or to thank your best customers and employees.

For more information, please visit us at:

www.simpletruths.com

or call us toll free …

800-900-3427